Coaching and Feedback Made Easy

2nd Edition

First Published 2010
Updated 2020

ISBN-13: 978-1453844380
ISBN-10: 1453844384

Derek Good
Auckland
New Zealand

Contents

Coaching and Feedback Made Easy

Foreword by Simon O'Shaughnessy

Derek's down to earth take on Coaching & Feedback is a great introduction to the art of coaching. It's practical and easy to engage but holds enough thoughts for a year of interaction.

Coaching opens the often untapped resource in any business - Empowered staff - staff that are engaged, creative, happy and flexible in their work.

Managers who extend themselves by learning to coach will open doors, and cross barriers, that others fail to see. And clients notice!

Simon O'Shaughnessy
Executive Coach and TEC Chair. Carista Ltd.

Simon is a top executive coach with over 35 years worth of business successes in the UK and Australasia. He currently advises and coaches a number of CEOs and business leaders as well as chair a branch of the 'The Executive Connection'.

Introduction

With a worldwide event like Covid-19, having the skills to coach people in different ways is essential. 2020 is a year that no one will forget in a hurry and the 'new' normal may take some time to define. One thing is for sure and that is skilled leaders with the ability to coach effectively will have a bigger positive impact than many other leadership skills.

There are three basic fundamentals that all people want to be able to do and these are exhibited continuously in the working environment. They want to achieve, contribute and learn. If you look at the surveys conducted about staff engagement and the lists of things that staff members want as top priorities in the workplace, it's these three areas that will come out on or near the top in almost all. Sure, everyone needs money to survive and live but that isn't the driving force. If it was, people would move jobs for 1% extra somewhere else. The reason they don't is because they are getting more than just monetary return for their efforts.

People aren't just working for pay in most cases. They have a vested interest in what they do and the organisations they work for. Managers could get so much more out of their staff if they just realised how to tap into the potential and energies that are there. Instead, some staff members are barely motivated to get into work let alone give their all to their roles.

This book takes a 'no nonsense' approach to coaching and feedback. It's not rocket science but it does take a little bit of common sense and some key skills to learn to be able to see how much more effective we can be in this area. Some people coach religiously and yet see no change in the behaviours of their people. We'll explain why this happens and how you can be the catalyst for change in your organisations through your people.

Coaching and feedback defined

Coaching is referred to as the activity of a coach in developing the abilities of coachees (people being coached). Coaching tends to focus on the achievement by coachees of a goal or a specific skill. We tend to coach others by giving them feedback.

For feedback to be valuable, it needs to be done right!

If I say "you are a great worker" or "you're fantastic" it is general and non-specific and does not mean much. Or if I say "You look sloppy today" or "You are not a good worker", you could feel upset and get defensive.

If we give non-specific feedback we'll often get a defensive response, like "what do you mean?"

There are different types of feedback. For the sake of keeping things simple, we shall refer to these in two types:

Encouraging and developmental

Although with both types of feedback, there are evaluative and descriptive phrases which are explained later in this chapter, these two are the two main types of feedback we shall refer to.

Encouraging feedback (sometimes known as reinforcing feedback) is designed to reinforce good behaviours exhibited by the coachee. This helps to show people that they are on the right track and is especially helpful if the behaviour (what they did or said) was linked to the outcome or result. A person will gain so much more from a conversation that doesn't just centre on WHAT they did but WHY they did it. Linking the WHY to the result will help reinforce the reasons for continuing (or stopping) a certain behaviour. Coaching is not cheerleading and leaders, managers and coaches must recognise the difference. Just saying 'you did a great job there' or 'that was excellent' will not reinforce strongly enough the behaviour you want them to continue using. It needs to be followed by a discussion on why is was a great job or why it was excellent and what the impact was on the outcome because of what they did or said.

In encouraging or reinforcing feedback, you would describe what has been done and discuss the impact it has had. For example, if a staff member resolved a query then explained to the customer that to save time on their next query they could register their query on the website and someone would call them back at a convenient time for them and the leader wanted to coach on that, the leader could say,

> *"When you offered that service to the customer about registering future queries that way, you really added some great value that they weren't expecting. It shows you understand the future needs of the customer extremely well. You didn't have to say it but you did and that customer has a better view of our company as a result. Great work. Keep it up."*

The staff member would feel acknowledged, reassured for giving the information and great about what they did as well as having the reasons reinforced by their leader. Everyone wins.

Developmental feedback (also known as corrective or constructive feedback) focuses on what they can improve on. This can also be done in a positive manner and is often avoided in poor coaching because coaches don't want to 'hurt feelings' or engage in conflict or are just not sure how to do it.

This is best done right before the person has an opportunity to use it. This means that it is often wasted at the end of the day for example as they will just be reflecting on the feedback and not on the impact it could have.

This type of feedback is well done if you are coaching someone live in a setting where you are taking calls together, making sales visits or in the work environment live. For example, if you wanted a staff member to try out a new technique to pause after asking for a sale, you could say,

> "Okay, on this next call, after you have asked them for the business, just pause and don't say anything until they speak next. Let them speak first okay?"

Once the staff member tries it out and sees the effect, they'll have additional confidence in what you've told them and keep using it. If you said it a week earlier, there's little chance they will remember to do it and therefore not reap any associated benefits.

In giving developmental feedback, it is important to help the coachee see things as facts rather than your opinion. Facts always mean that there is something concrete and less to argue over. The developmental feedback then should be descriptive rather than evaluative. Descriptive feedback focuses on stating the facts while evaluative feedback focuses on your opinion.

Here are some examples:

Act: Person comes to work without a name badge on:

Evaluative Feedback: "You're sloppy"

Descriptive Feedback: "You don't have your name badge on"

Act: Person comes into work ten minutes late:

Evaluative Feedback: "You don't care about your work very much"

Descriptive Feedback: "I see you are late this morning"

Act: Person shouts across the office

Evaluative Feedback: "You got really angry back then"

Descriptive Feedback: "You raised your voice in that conversation"

You can see that the descriptive feedback can then lead you into a proper discussion about the behaviour exerted. Evaluative feedback could lead the other person to disagree with you and argue another reason for the behaviour.

Motivation to be coached

For people to be able to do something well, they need to have three things:

1. Knowledge of what to do
2. Skills for performing the task
3. A desire to do it

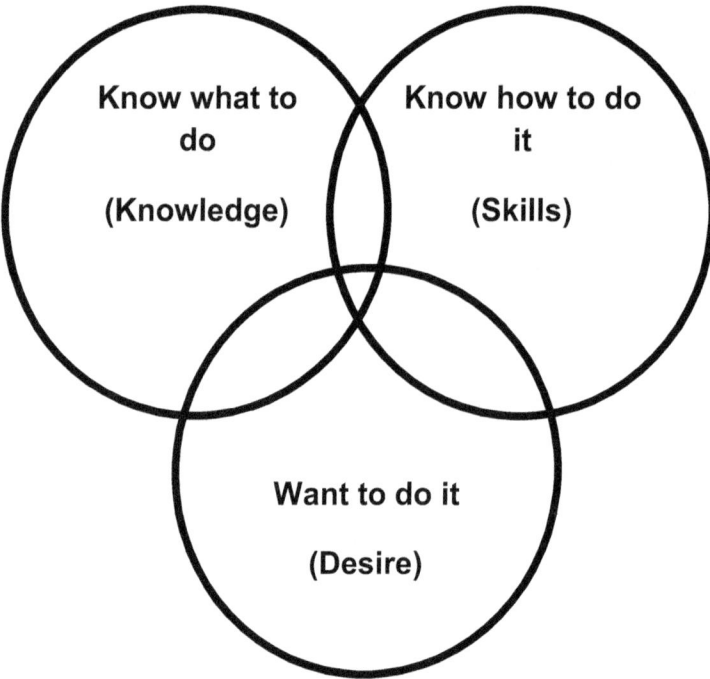

Fig 1. Three requirements

It's no good just having one or two of those things – all three are needed in order to get the best result.

When you're motivated to do something, you will be much more likely to accomplish it faster and more efficiently than when you're not. Motivation is our driving force. We are all motivated by different things and when we find ourselves 'in flow' where the time just whizzes by, we know that we are motivated in doing what we are doing.

Unless the person being coached wants to change or listen to you, it's unlikely that anything will change at all. The person needs to have the desire to change. People try all sorts of methods to motivate staff members and coaching is no different. What we really want is for the coachee to want to change their behaviour or to want to do what it is we are recommending. If we take the various motivation options, we could put them into a simple matrix (see Fig 2):

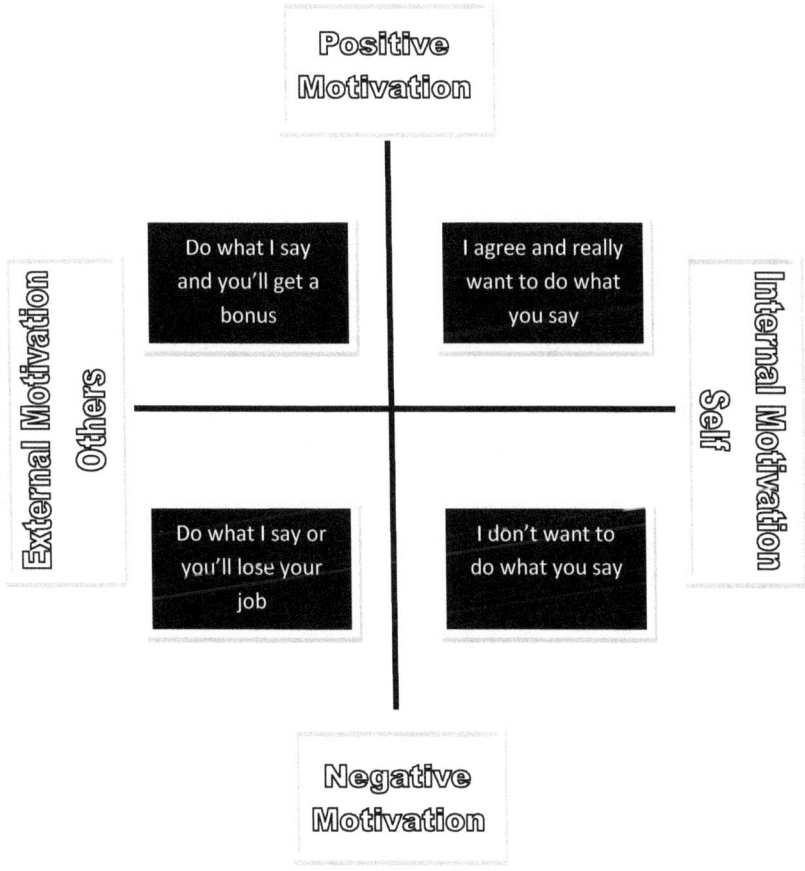

Fig 2. Motivation matrix

Basically, unless the person wants to change or do what's required, the likelihood is that they won't! Using negative motivation (for example - do it or you're fired!) may only gain a short term positive response. Like any external motivation, once the external motivation has gone, so has the desire. Even with positive motivation – if it's externally pushed (for example - do it and you'll get a prize) will mean that when the prize is no longer there, the desire has gone too. You'll have to keep providing prizes to keep up the motivation and the chances are, you'll have to start increasing the perceived value of the prizes to keep their interest. Oh, and by the way, their salary is not considered enough of a prize in most cases.

This motivation using positive and negative consequences is a fascinating topic and you may like to research a bit more. Try searching articles on 'Operant Conditioning' if you would like to know more.

WHY not WHAT

The real winner for motivation is to help create an internal desire to perform the task, make the change or act in the way you want them to. Now that's easier said than done but there are some key principles you can use in order to impact on this result. Firstly, understand what drives the individual in the first place. What pushes their buttons? What are their interests? The more you know about them, the easier it will be to tie in a motivator to their role or task.

As an example, one person – we'll call her Mary - was struggling to be motivated to do her role. She worked for a government department in a call centre. Her great love was opera singing. How on earth was the manager going to find a link to help motivate her to improve her interactions with callers? During the discussion, the manager started to focus on the 'WHY' rather than the 'WHAT'.

So often we spend our energies talking about what people like to do and what motivates rather than why we like to do it or why it motivates them. During this discussion, Mary explained that she loved the way she made people feel after performing opera. They felt better somehow, lifted and happier. Once the manager got this information, she was able to help Mary see that by doing her job well, she could also make people feel better, lifted and happier by dealing with their queries and helping them resolve any issues. That was it! That was all Mary needed to get going and perform. She had discovered a link between what motivated her and her job.

Getting this right will help you get buy-in from the individual. Buy-in means that you see the benefits and want to proceed with it 100%. It's more than supporting the idea and certainly more than accepting it. We all accept the price of petrol – because we pay it – but I don't think we all have buy-in for the price it is set at. We're not eagerly queuing up to fill our tanks the minute we see the needle dip just below full – we're more likely to drive to the near-limit of the tank before we grudgingly go to the petrol pumps. Support for something means that we will tell people it's a good idea. We see some benefits. We might pay a contribution to a cause because we support it but we might not be up at 4am to join in the protest march or do without the new TV and donate all the money.

It's not until we really get behind something – live and breathe it, see that it's the only way and drive ourselves there without the need for someone else that we have buy-in. When the manager has left for the day, we continue on as normal because we are internally motivated to do so. We are not relying on the manager watching us to perform at our best.

Effective coaching

Coaching is about carrying, transporting or moving somebody from one state or place to another. It is really about helping people resolve their own issues and discover their own potential. Coaching is not about lecturing or telling people what to do or solving all their problems. Although you may need to instruct or direct from time to time, the major role of a coach is to help the coachee find the solution themselves. This method of self-discovery is a fundamental leadership skill and can make all the difference.

If you believe you are coaching someone else because you are more capable than the other person, you are looking at coaching incorrectly. In many cases, the person being coached will know more about the systems, processes, products, services and even customers than you will. It's not about being the hero or the rescuer. It's not about looking smart or showing that you know everything. It's about helping people know how to come to solutions on their own, develop strategies for a better way of thinking and facilitating issues so they have total ownership.

You can do all this by developing your own questioning, listening and paraphrasing skills. As a coach, you need to develop skills in 'drawing' information out of people.

The aim of good coaching is to facilitate a discussion. This means that your task is to 'draw out' information from the person you are coaching. It's about helping them discover themselves the answers and solutions. Self-discovery is a term to be aware of as a leader. Use it to ensure you are not just lecturing or telling people what to do.

Coaching the right way

In order to coach the right way, we need to understand what the wrong way is. Let's face it, we have all had some experience where coaching hasn't been very effective. In fact, I have had organisations say to me that they have regular coaching but nothing changes. Their leaders coach each month, people commit and then hold the same conversations the next month again with no change. This is a classic example of coaching on activators in order to change behaviours.

Activators are those items that cause us to do something. In themselves they have some motivation behind them. For example, an activator we all have is hunger. This activator leads us to do a certain behaviour which is to feed ourselves. This behaviour leads to a consequence which is that we become full (or put on weight)!

So, there are three components in this process:

- The **activator** is the driver of the behaviour.

- The **behaviour** is what is done.

- The **consequence** is the result.

Coaching that is focused on the activator is less effective. This is coaching that focuses on words like, "do more, do better, faster, increase, slow down, improve" etc. people then under pressure or wishing to please say, "Okay". Leaders then feel they have a commitment and are surprised that the behaviour hasn't changed. They then coach more and say the same stuff but louder, bolder etc.

However, if the consequence is changed, the behaviour is much more likely to be altered. Think about these two examples:

1. If you were thirsty (activator) and you put $2 in a drinks machine (behaviour) you would expect a drink (consequence). However, if the drink did not come out as a result, you are not likely to keep putting $2 in the machine. The consequence is dramatically different that it has changed your behaviour. You are more likely to kick the machine or call someone up about it rather than keep putting money in.

2. If the room got dark as a result of the sun going down (activator) and you turned the light switch on (behaviour) you would expect the light to come on (consequence). However, if the light did not work, you would not keep turning the light switch on (apart from that frantic on/off pressing until you realised it won't work). You would source an alternative light source like a torch.

So, you can see that with these two examples, the change in the consequence made a huge impact on the actual behaviour exhibited.

Now think about your people and their roles. What example can you start with where you want behaviour to change? What is the activator and the normal consequence? What can you change the consequence to be in order for the behaviour to change?

Some coaching is done to tick a box. I.e. a leader feels they must coach so they do (not very well) and tick the coaching box. Coaching is not a passive action; it needs to be engaging, thought through and personal to the individual. You cannot hope to coach everybody the same way. People in your team will have preferences and needs that vary.

The brain and coaching

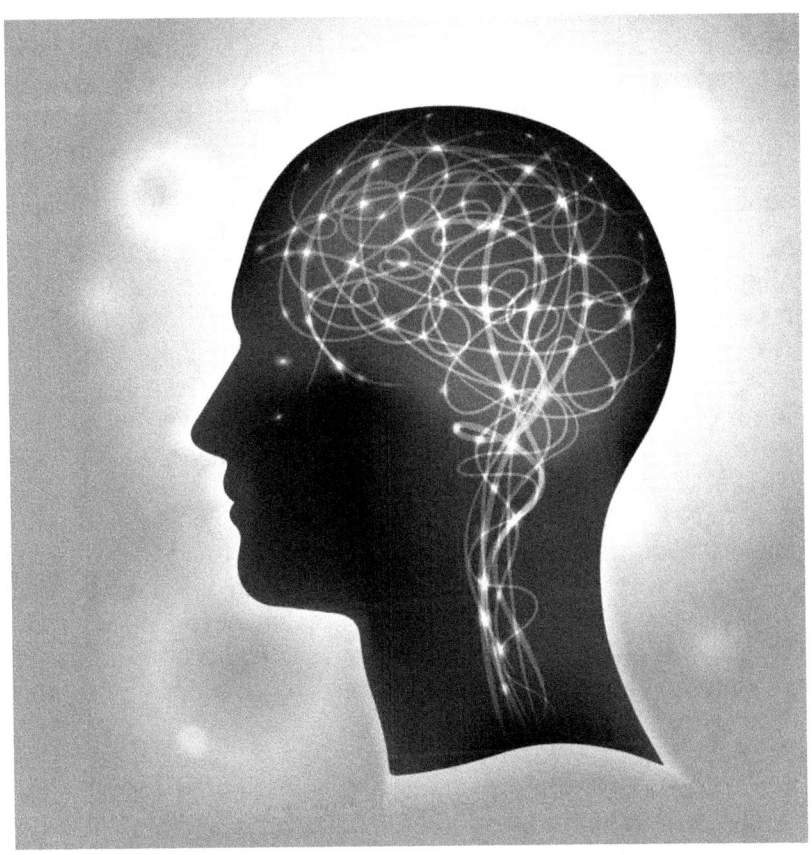

When the brain is exposed to a new stimulus of any type – image, smell, voice, sensation etc, there is a lot of activity. Neurons are firing all over the brain as it searches for some recognition or place of reference for the stimulus. Eventually, it will store the stimulus somewhere for accessing again. The second time the brain encounters the same stimulus, there is still a lot of activity but not as much as the brain locates the initial stored stimulus and then there is recognition. Third and subsequent times, the brain more quickly accesses the stored information and eventually, the stimulus creates a 'hard wired'

reaction where the brain doesn't have to run through much accessing but knows where to find the response that's generally required for that stimulus.

Those hard wired reactions are what we call habitual. They are automatic pilot responses and ways of dealing with things. Each of us develops these 'hard wired' reactions over time for lots of things. At work, we become quite proficient in what we do because we have 'hard wired' the processes. Very often, we don't have to think too hard about all that we do – it's automatic. Our staff too have this 'hard wiring' going on when they do things such as talking to customers, habits for the way they talk to customers, methods they use to shortcut the systems they use, responses they rely on to deal with situations etc.

Some of those habits however aren't what we want to see or are not the way they should be approaching their work. Our job then is to break that hard wiring and help them to find new routes in the brain. This can be quite hard. Think of a habit you have that you have tried to break. It's not that easy is it? Unless you have a better alternative or some driving desire, you probably won't change. However, sometimes you do change. Why is that? Well, think about it this way. You probably have a favourite restaurant or holiday spot. That only became your favourite after someone introduced it to you or you were exposed to it. Before then, some other place was your favourite. For us then in coaching, we need to expose our coachees to other alternatives; ideas that can lead them to substitute their current habit for a new one. One that will improve their performance, reaction from customers or whatever it is we are coaching them on.

Just like the example of motivation, we don't do that by externally imposing something. We know that doesn't work. We need to create an internal motivation to change.

So, tapping in to a person's motivation is the sure way to get them to improve performance, correct mistakes and sustain the change. There are ten basic principles for coaching and feedback success that we'll now discuss.

Why coach?

Coaching is really about helping people resolve their own issues and discover their own potential. Coaching is not about lecturing or telling people what to do or solving all their problems. Although you may need to instruct or direct from time to time, the major role of a coach is to help the coachee find the solution themselves.

If you believe you are coaching someone else because you are more capable than the other person, you are looking at coaching incorrectly. In many cases, the person being coached will know more about the systems, processes, products, services and even customers than you will. It's not about being the hero or the rescuer. It's not about looking smart or showing that you know everything. It's about helping people know how to come to solutions on their own, develop strategies for a better way of thinking and facilitating issues so they have total ownership.

You can do all this by developing your own questioning, listening and paraphrasing skills (see later section on communication). As a coach, you need to develop skills in 'drawing' information out of people.

So, what are the purposes of coaching? Well, there are many reasons to coach – here's a few:

Development: Develop further understanding or skills of others

Facilitate: Help others discover new ways of doing things, resolve issues and identify fixes

Training: Up skill in new areas and techniques

Correct mistakes:	Help identify errors and change those behaviours
Give praise:	Encourage others and congratulate them on good work, consistent good behaviour, results that have exceeded expectation etc
Delegate:	Help develop others through delegation
Regulate:	Achieve consistency through standards followed up by coaching

Trust

When you are coaching – especially if you have moved to a more remote environment, you may feel less involved and worry about what your team members are doing. You may struggle to trust them. Don't be tempted to tell them that they need to build trust with you. Start by trusting them. Start by explaining to them that you are confident in their abilities to do the job. Don't micro-manage. Just set up 'check ins' to make sure they are okay and establish parameters around outcomes rather than tasks. You will motivate them much more through giving them your trust rather than making them earn it.

Use outcomes – 'what has to be done by when' to measure how they are doing. Give them freedom and trust. If they break the trust, then you can coach them to improve their performance and talk about consequences – good and bad for what happens next.

The 10 key principles of effective coaching

Although there are many principles of quality coaching techniques, there are some that will have the biggest impact on those being coached and the effectiveness of the experience for both parties. Consider the following ten principles as those that have been 'boiled down' for maximum impact for your coaching success. Consider always that we are all on a quest to continuously learn and adapt, so don't stop your research in to ways and techniques that can improve your style, strengthen your approach and increase your abilities as a coach.

Principle 1: Coach the individual

The first basic for coaching is to realise that each person is different and they will require some individual attention and approach in regards to feedback and coaching. Some people will be very sensitive and embarrassed to be given constructive feedback and may need some confidence boosting first while others will want to dispense with any pleasantries and get straight into areas of improvement. You can't treat these two extremes the same.

There isn't just one model of feedback and one way of coaching that works but there are plenty that don't.

In order to know how to approach each person, you need to know a bit about them. What type of learning style do they have? What is their personality type? What do they like to do in their spare time? Who do they hang around with at work? What are some of the strengths you have noticed about them? What makes them smile? Why do they work where they do? These are just a few of the questions that knowing the answer to will help you in your role as a coach.

If you know their best learning style (audio, visual or kinaesthetic), you will know how best to approach your coaching with them. For audio preferences you can ensure that you engage in good discussion, play back a recorded call to them if possible, get them to listen to a good and bad example of a conversation etc. For visual learners, write things down, show them graphs, trends or diagrams and keep plenty of colour going. Show them things on the computer screen and describe things by way of the 'big picture' – how does what they do impact on the rest of the organisation or the customer. For kinaesthetic preferences, ensure that they are involved doing something. Don't just show them – let them do it. Practice doing role plays and have them offer suggestions. These people learn best by doing.

So how do you know which preference your people have? You can run a simple AVK test (there are loads of free ones on the internet). You can listen to the way they talk – do they use audio language (I hear what you're saying, that sounds great etc) or visual language (I see what you mean, I can't see where this is going, I can picture that etc) or Kinaesthetic language (I feel for you, it just doesn't feel right etc). Or you can just simply ask them what they prefer – it can be that simple!

Personality styles can also provide you with clues as to how people like to be coached and receive feedback. Some people like recognition – so you can get them to accept challenges with a promise of such. Some people want to avoid conflict, so approach the situation by putting them at ease etc.

In short, you need to come of the 'auto pilot' and be in a conscious state when coaching. You can't assume that everyone is happy with your standard default approach and remember that each individual is just that – an individual who needs their kind of attention. The golden rule states that you should treat people as you wish to be treated. Well that's not going to work in coaching and feedback sessions. You need to live the platinum rule which is to treat people as <u>they</u> wish to be treated.

Tip: Get to know the person you are coaching. Ask them their preferences. If they're not sure, give them some options.

Principle 2: Know several ways to coach

As a coach and knowing the key point about coaching others as individuals means that you then need to have several tools in your toolkit of ways to effectively coach and give feedback. It's impossible to coach everyone the way they need to be coached with one dimensional coaching abilities. It's your role to look for, learn and master several coaching skills and feedback techniques.

There isn't one right way to coach and the more techniques you learn, the better equipped you'll be to coach more diverse people. The key though is not knowing more ways to coach on its own, it's knowing which ones to use and when.

In this chapter, we will look at a couple of feedback models. You can also look at the chapter dealing with formal and informal coaching for more ideas on this.

Feedback models are important as they give some structure around giving feedback. Here we will look at two models (4 steps process and DESCCO).

4 steps process: Ask, Tell, Ask, Tell

Step 1: In this process, as the coach you direct the conversation by first asking them a question such as: "What do you think went well in that sales call?" You then listen to the individual share their thoughts on the matter.

Step 2: Next, you tell them what you think went well in that sales call. It may be that you confirm what they have said and elaborate a little more. People like to hear specifics about things. Think about the time you may have spoken at an event, written a report or performed on stage. If someone comes up to you and says, "Great job – I really enjoyed what you did!" Well, you feel good about it – but how much better and more sincere does it sound when someone adds something like, "I especially liked it when you did xxx". Adding that little bit of extra information helps you feel that they took something in, that it meant something to them and that they were attentive.

Step 3: You follow up your comments by asking another question based around what they think they would do differently next time. As an example, "what would you do differently if you could do it over?" or "what do you think you could improve on next time?" these questions are not negatively geared. The first example especially only asks for 'different' not 'better'. When people feel like the pressure is off a bit and don't have to come up with something better, just different it's much easier.

Step 4: Finally, you tell them what they could do differently. Again, you may confirm what they have said, or you may elaborate further.

This simple four steps process is a model that can be used to engage people in conversation and gets them thinking about what they have done and ways to look at it differently.

In summary, the Four Step Process is:

Step One: **Ask them what went well**

Step Two: **Tell them what you thought went well**

Step Three: **Ask them what they could have done differently**

Step Four: **Tell them what you think they could have done differently**

To enhance this experience further, you may also like to add some other questions at each step. Ensure that the questions have some meaning and make a point and also add value. For example, after any of the responses, you could ask something like, "And what impact might that have had on the customer?" Getting them to think about the consequence of the responded action will help further embed reasoning into what they or you have said.

Here's how the whole conversation could go. Let's take a phone coaching situation where the coach is listening in on a double headset. It could just as easily be a situation where a sales manager has joined one of their sales team on a series of sales calls face to face with customers.

Coach: "Okay John, what do you think you did well on that call?"

Customer Rep: "Well, I certainly solved the query she had and I think she went away happy. I also feel like I spoke clearly so she could understand"

Coach: "Yes, I think she certainly got the answer she needed and won't need to call back for anything and I like the way you got her to paraphrase back your answer to make sure she understood. Great. Now what could you have done differently?"

Customer Rep: "Ummm, I'm not sure."

Coach: "Thinking about the way you addressed the person, is there anything you could have changed?"

Customer Rep: "Oh, do you mean about the way I used 'Madam'?"

Coach: "Yes, that's right. At the start of the call, she called herself Mrs Garcia twice which indicated that her preference for addressing her is that way. How do you think using the customer's name like that might have changed the way the call went?"

Customer Rep:	"Well, I suppose it would have made it more personal."
Coach:	"That's right, it would. When you call companies, do you like to be treated personally?"
Customer Rep:	"Well, yes, I suppose I do."
Coach:	"Ok then. Let's look at that on the next call. I think that will make quite a difference from the customer perspective."

There are so many ways to conduct this type of feedback model. You may like to change it around a bit to: ASK, ASK, TELL, TELL. You may even want to just ASK. The important thing is to get the individual to talk, keep it specific and help them during the conversation to get to the points you want them to make where necessary.

DESCCO

The second feedback model to explain to you is the DESCCO method. Here, we have an acronym for the words:

Describe the behaviour

Express how you felt

Specify what you'd prefer

Consequences of the new action

Contract to act in the new way

Ok

Like the Ask Tell process above, there are many ways to use the DESCCO model. Firstly, if you wanted to give direct feedback to someone say for shouting across a room, you might use it like this:

"John, when you shouted across the office, I felt like you distracted everyone else from their work. If you want my attention, I'd prefer it if you walked over to my office and spoke with me. That way, you won't be disturbing everybody else and potentially distracting them in their work flow. So, can I expect you to not shout next time you want me for something? Okay."

So, you'll see in that short paragraph that we used all the steps of DESCCO in a simple flow:

Describe: "When you shouted across the office…"

Express: "I felt like you distracted everyone else from their work."

Specify: "I'd prefer it if you walked over to my office…"

Consequences: "That way, you won't be disturbing everybody…"

Contract: "So, can I expect you to not shout…"

Ok: "Okay."

Each of the steps has an important element to play in helping people to alter their behaviour. Firstly, describing what they did helps the person know exactly what it is you're talking about. It's therefore much more useful if the feedback given is descriptive (i.e. factual). The expression component then personalises it and gives some meaning to the effect of their behaviour. Specifying another way of approaching it gives them an alternative and explaining the consequences (which could be good or bad) gives reasoning for the person to consider the new behaviour suggestion. The contract is a way of getting them to concur or show their understanding. The ending with 'Okay' is for them to agree.

In our example above, we have shown a direct 'telling' method of giving feedback. Of course, it can be even more powerful if you switch the 'telling' to 'asking' in each of the steps of the DESCCO process after the 'Describe' step. For example, "When you shouted across the office, what impact do you think that had on the rest of the team?" This way you will be able to uncover their understanding and thinking a lot sooner and potentially gain greater buy-in. This method is discussed in greater depth in Principle 4: Encourage Self Discovery.

There are many models for giving feedback. Some people won't want you to go through a process like the four steps – they may prefer just to be told what they need to do to improve. It's therefore very important that Principle 1: Coach the individual is adhered to in the first instance and find out how they best respond to coaching.

> **Tip:** Learn a few coaching and feedback models like Ask Tell and DESCCO. Practice them at home on family or with friends. Do some role plays with someone you are comfortable with.

Principle 3: Don't just tick boxes

Several people have said to me in the past, "Well, we do coaching regularly but nothing changes." Going back to the section on motivation, most people see the need for coaching, so they do it but for a lot of people, the coach isn't converted. The coach doesn't have buy-in and at best 'accepts' that it needs to be done. The problem isn't with the coachee – it's with the coach! These might be harsh words – but they are true (in most cases).

One of the big traps to fall into is to get into a routine of doing something because it should be done. In a lot of cases, it might as well never be done for all the benefit that comes. Coaching is not a register. It's not a checklist. If our approach is all about making sure we coach a certain number of times and cover off the minimum number of points, we have done just that – we might have achieved our goal (coaching each team member every two weeks say) but our objective to help people improve performance has been missed by a mile.

So, when coaching, we need to have a purpose. Ask yourself the question, "What is it I really want to see as a result of this coaching session?" or "What will tell me this session has been worthwhile?" or even "What do I want to see next for this person?" Have a purpose, have a reason for the coaching session to go ahead. This might need some planning time. Be prepared. The coachee deserves a bit of preparation. Sure, they need to be engaged too – but the onus is on you as the coach to run the session and direct the result.

Look to make the change in the individual. Rather than closing the session wondering if anything will be different from then on – have the goal that something *will* be different by the end of the session. Of course, this means you need to have some focus on what would be reasonable, what needs to change, how can you help the individual see the benefits of changing and how will you know that they are on board with it all. Well a lot of that will depend on your preparation or observation skills and on how you run the session.

Think about the times you have had a change of mind or found something new and from then on run with it. What about a restaurant that you love or a meal that's become your favourite? Perhaps it is a new item of clothing, a movie, a book or a holiday destination. All of these things would once have been introduced to you at some point. Now before that time, something else was your favourite meal, your favourite movie etc. Now, however, it's all different because you have changed you preference. You have had a new experience; you've seen something different in it that makes you prefer to do, say, eat or experience that over other options. That's the sort of experience we should look to create with our coachees.

Rather than just ticking boxes, work at having effective conversations. What will make a change in this individual? How can I get them to really think about consequences (good or bad) for doing something? What impact will their behaviour have on the customer, their job or their colleagues? The sorts of questions we can look at in the following section will be ideal places to start where we look at how to Encourage Self Discovery.

Tip: Before you begin coaching, consider what you really want this person to get out of the session. If you're not sure before you start, take time before you conclude to sum up and get a firm action from them.

Principle 4: Encourage self-discovery

There are varying schools of thought on what ratio the coaching discussion should go in regards to the amount of talking from each party. It wouldn't be too far off the mark though to suggest 70:30 in favour of the coachee, where the coach effectively facilitates the discussion to draw out information and suggestions from the coachee.

Sometimes as coaches, we feel that we have the knowledge and the fastest and best way to share it is to tell, tell, tell. Consider the effectiveness of that ideology. The old adage goes:

If you tell me, I'll probably forget
If you show me I might remember
If you involve me, I'll understand

When we get involved, we not only stand a better chance of remembering something, we also get to understand why and how it all works. Think about a time you needed directions to drive somewhere. If you were told directions, you may have struggled your way there and even got a little lost on the way. If you were a passenger, you have a better chance of remembering the route BUT if you drove there yourself, you will more likely remember the route best.

Learning a new skill takes involvement. You can read all you like about how to swim – but until you get into the water – you won't actually learn.

So, the ability to get the other person to try and figure out an answer or solution will help them immensely over just telling them. We all benefit more when we have had to struggle a bit. The result is more valuable to us. We had to earn it. By the same token though, don't leave them floundering. If they need a nudge – help them in the right direction.

We looked at the DESCCO method earlier on. Rather than using the direct tell, tell, tell approach we first looked at, how about asking the individual the questions? Flip it round a bit. For example, let's say you wanted to address the issue that they had shouted across the office to get someone's attention. You could start by addressing the behaviour thus, "When you shouted across the office...how do you think it made everybody else feel?" This covers off the 'Describe' and 'Express' components of DESCCO. But, rather than you telling them how it made you or others felt – you have asked them to put themselves in others' shoes.

Then go to the next step and 'specify' by asking "What would have been another way to handle that?" Let them answer and encourage them where needed. Then follow up with the 'consequences' "And what might be the result of that?" You are likely to get a response that will just need a confirmation from you and you can finish off with "Exactly, so next time you need to get hold of someone quickly, will you do it that way?" Ok.

You don't have to use the DESCCO method – that's just an example but get them to think. You don't have to show them you know everything by telling them – you can show them by asking them and confirming if you like – that way you don't sound like your force feeding them but helping them see that they know the answers already themselves.

If they just aren't getting it and need some help, be more specific. Let's say you were coaching someone on a conversation they had and you asked them how they could improve and they couldn't think of anything, ask a follow up question about the specific area of the conversation. If the ending was bad – ask them how they could improve the ending.

The best way to get buy-in from someone else is to help them come up with the idea or at least help them think it was their idea. Draw out of the individual what they think is acceptable or right or the best way to handle something. This method of coaching or working with people is known as facilitation. It can be defined as the act of assisting or making easier the progress or improvement of something. Normally, facilitation would be used in the context of a group where the facilitator would be there to help the group to have an effective dialog without taking any side of the argument, especially in order to reach a consensus. In a one-on-one situation, the facilitator, or coach, can also be there to help guide the discussion effectively to a certain destination.

In essence, the self discovery component focuses on helping the individual being coached to come up with a reasonable response or suggestion that they can own. They may need some guidance but you should avoid giving them the answers or jumping straight into the 'telling' mode unless absolutely necessary.

Tip: Getting the other person to talk is the key. Ask questions and avoid 'telling'. When you feel like you're about to give the solution, ask a question about it first.

Principle 5: Look for the cause

Most of us will have been to the doctor in order to be diagnosed for a cure to be given for a number of symptoms we have. You will have noticed on a trip to the doctors or hospital that you will have been asked a number of questions. These questions are designed to help determine the cause of the symptoms that you have. Let's say you have constant headaches. There could be lots of causes for those headaches but if the doctor merely prescribed a headache tablet for example, it may not cure you of the headaches ongoing. The doctor's job is to identify what is causing the headaches and treat that cause – not just the symptom.

The popular TV series in the late 2000's called 'House' is an ideal example of how the doctors have to find the actual cause of the symptoms displayed. If they don't identify the root cause, the treating of the symptoms would be often fruitless and pointless.

In your role as a coach, one of the key aspects is to try to uncover the reasons why somebody may not be doing what they should. The skills of using self discovery could be very useful here.

Let's take an example here of someone not using your knowledge base to look up information for a customer when it is obvious to you that it may help give valuable information. To you, that may be just fundamental in order to service the customer. You may be tempted to just tell the person to start using it. After all, it's there and it's useful. If, however, the person is a little phobic when it comes to computers, they may not want to use it. Maybe they haven't had enough training on it. Perhaps they have used it in the past and it didn't really help them. They may have tried using it and find it very slow and therefore a hindrance when talking to the customer. Any one of these or perhaps other reasons could exist and each one will require a different tact in dealing with the issue – as follows:

Reason	Action
Don't like computers	Give them some training
Didn't help in the past	Review the example and share personal experience. Look for something that's helped you
System too slow	Jump on the system with them and see for yourself – get them to show you. Report to IT
Not sure how to use it	Show them. Give them some scheduled training

Treating the cause will alleviate the issues faced with frustration because you feel like you keep telling someone but they don't change.

As an opportunity to practice this, ask the individual the two main reasons they can see why they don't do something. If they struggle to come up with an answer – give them a couple of options. Then ask the important question, "If we could fix that, would you do it?" – (or the equivalent relevant question).

Tip: Avoid the temptation to act on the first response. Dig a little deeper for the root cause.

Principle 6: Be present and focus

One of the four main principles of the FISH! Philosophy established by John Christensen is 'Be There' or 'Be Present' which has more to do with giving your full attention to a task or individual. We expect our staff members to focus on their tasks - especially when they are engaged with customers, so it's right that we are focusing on the individuals in coaching. We may feel that we can multitask but let's face it; some multi tasking is just like being all over the place.

In order for us to fully comprehend our staff and to catch all the nuances and potential reasons behind their statements etc we need to give them our full attention. At the very least, it's common courtesy to be fully engaged in a coaching session anyway. If we aren't prepared to listen intently or if we allow ourselves to drift into 'auto pilot' because we've 'heard this all before' or we 'think' we know where this is going, then we may miss something vital.

There are some famous words penned by the Georgian poet, William Henry Davies, "No matter where this body is, the mind is free to go elsewhere." We can be physically present but mentally far away from what we're actually doing. We've all experienced trying to get someone's attention and not got it completely or we've been in a conversation and noticed a pause when we weren't really paying attention and then had the awful feeling of knowing that we were just asked a question and never heard it. It's a little embarrassing and it certainly isn't professional.

Even if we are having the coaching session but we're trying to finish something off first. It's not giving the other person the right signals to make them wait as we are effectively saying that something else is more important than them.

If we want our teams to get switched on to coaching and look forward to it. We need to create the best possible environment and best experience we can for them so that even developmental feedback is a positive experience.

> **Tip:** Stop what else you're doing. Physically turn away from your desk and give the person your full attention. Establish eye contact.

Principle 7: Give direction

This principle may be one that sounds obvious. Of course we need to give direction. We don't want to take away from the individuals though and their opportunity to think for themselves so you'll notice that this follows on from the principle of self discovery.

Being a coach or a leader means that you need to ensure the individual goes away with something specific they can do. They don't just need encouragement – although that's important. If encouragement was all that was required, you could be a cheerleader instead of a team leader. Telling someone they're doing ok or that something wasn't too bad doesn't actually give them any help as to how to make it better or how to improve.

Let's take an example here. Say you were blindfolded and were trying to throw paper balls into a waste paper basket. If the person watching you just said things like: "Not bad", "Ohhh that was close", "Nice try", "Good". Does that actually tell you anything constructive towards getting the paper in the basket? Not really. It may sound encouraging and you may feel like you're on the right track but being on the right track isn't good enough if you really want to get the paper in the basket. You need phrases like: "Try it three inches to the left", "Just about an inch higher", You keep hitting the left hand rim". These phrases actually give you something to work with. They are directions.

Again, if you wanted to get somewhere specific, you would naturally ask directions (unless you're like me. In which case you will exhaust every possible hunch you have about where to go first!) When someone gives you directions, they give you specific instructions to follow. It's not a game of 'hot' and 'cold' – it's specific statements about where to go in order to reach a destination.

Likewise, while coaching, you need to ensure that your instructions are specific and direct and not ambiguous.

Tip: Avoid adjectives like 'nearly there'. Focus on specific instructions. Treat it like a recipe or a list of directions to go somewhere or how to operate a piece of equipment.

Principle 8: Change their perspective

Sometimes people struggle to 'get it' from the customer perspective. You obviously get it. Why don't they? This is a common issue that's faced. Part of the problem with this principle is that people haven't experienced what the customer is experiencing and find themselves with absolutely no empathy for the situation at all. This is especially evident when young people are employed and are serving customers in areas that they have no experience in. Take for example power companies. A school leaver dealing with customers in a power company may have never paid a power bill, don't know why it costs so much and has no idea of budgeting for it.

It's important therefore to focus on something they will have some idea about or some relationship to. For example, if you're trying to get across a point about the way they spoke to a customer, you may try to turn things round a bit and ask: "If that customer was your mother, would you be happy with the way she was treated?" Or "If you were on your lunch break and waited 15 minutes in a bank queue only to hear the person in front of you at the counter talk about the weekend sport – would you be happy about that?"

The trick is to find a scenario that will allow them to tap into their way of thinking and turn it around. What would make sense to them? What is the equivalent in their language or their world?

A simple way to look at this is to role play with them. You take on the role of the company and let them be the customer. Then run a scenario similar to the one you are trying to get them to improve. Don't take any prisoners either. Help them see how unreasonable, difficult, crazy it may sound like to them.

Tip: Put the individual in the shoes of the customer or try to turn the customer into someone that they care about such as a family member or a good friend.

Principle 9: Use positive language

Your staff will mimic you. I have noticed when videoing coaching sessions in the past that the person being coached ends up talking similarly to the person who is coaching. Sometimes, people actually start using the exact same words.

We want our staff to be confident and positive with our customers so we need to be examples of that when we are talking with them. There's no doubt that as customers we want to feel confident in the person who we are speaking with. Imagine what it would be like if we asked our insurance company if something was covered under the policy and they replied, "I think so" or "It should be". Those types of responses do not create a feeling of safety or peace of mind. We expect to hear things like "Yes it does" or "No it doesn't, but it does cover you for xxx".

Imagine if you went to the doctors and you were given some medication and you asked if it would help with a particular ailment and all you got was the doctor shrugging their shoulders. You just wouldn't bother taking the medication would you? What would be the point?

Some of the words that we use don't support the positive, confident environment we want to portray. Avoid using words like, 'should, maybe, possibly, perhaps'. All these words leave questions about the situation. Some people try to soften sentences by using these words as preambles. Just don't do it. Be confident. One great way to improve on this yourself is to practice. Record yourself and listen to the types of words you use. These 'wishy washy' words often come out when we are in a conflict situation and would rather not be. It may take a little time to eradicate them in your coaching sessions and the best way is to be conscious of them. Listen to yourself and catch yourself when you say them. Of course – they may be necessary in some instances. I've just used the word 'may' twice in this paragraph. Just make sure that they're used correctly and not thrown in for good measure.

> **Tip:** Make a list of negative sounding words and practice not using them. Work on words you can use as substitutes.

Principle 10: Keep it simple

It's the old adage of K.I.S.S. – keep it simple stupid. The more we load up our staff, the less likely they are of completing any of it. Think about trying to keep a shopping list in your head. By the time you get to the supermarket – it's gone or morphed into some other list. If you're anything like me, by the time you've ended your shop, your basket or trolley is full of stuff not on your original list. The brain just doesn't work well with keeping lists of things to do but works very well when there are just one or two things to focus on.

When you're coaching someone, there may be a list of 10 or 12 things that they need to work on. Forget it. That's just not practical. Get them to focus on the one or two things that will make the biggest impact in their role or to their performance. The likelihood is that if they fix those things, some of the others will fall into place as a result anyway. If the list of areas to work on is too long, they will just not know where to start. It's best to fix a couple of things, get them embedded then work on a couple more.

Tip: When you have your list of things for the person to work on, pick 1, 2 or 3 things at the most that will make the biggest impact for them and the business. Look for a quick win where you can. It will encourage them to do more.

Communication

It's the basis for how we interact with one another. We have some fantastic tools to help us communicate. These tools are not communication themselves. For example, talking and listening are tools for communicating but don't necessarily add up to communication. For example, if one person spoke in German and the other person didn't understand German – then they are not really communicating.

Communication is the **"exchange of understanding"**. It is the sharing of information where both parties understand one another. Tools to help in that exchange of understanding include:

- talking (through questioning and statements)
- listening
- paraphrasing
- body language

Listening skills

To be a good coach, you need to be a good listener. Here are some of the poor listening skills areas to be aware of. Take a pen and mark a 'Yes' or a 'No' next to each one that best indicates your answer.

1. I anticipate what people will say next as they are speaking
2. I'm constantly judging the merit of what people say from the very first sentence
3. I discount what other people say if they don't agree with my opinions and values
4. I rarely pay attention to people's non verbal cues (such as body language or facial expressions)
5. I prepare what I'm going to say in response while the other person is still talking
6. If I disagree with people, I interrupt them immediately to set the record straight
7. If the other person is long winded or boring, I stop listening
8. When I know what people are going to say, I don't wait for them to finish but answer right away
9. When I stop paying attention to someone I try to look like I'm listening anyway
10. I often interrupt people to speed along a conversation

So, how did you do? Obviously in this test, the more 'negative responses you have the better listener you are. For most people, getting half of these as 'No' would be a great result. Listening is a skill. It's an area we need to practice to get better like most other skills.

Think about this yourself and what you find yourself doing in conversations. In coaching it should be no different. You want to avoid being automatically ready with your response when the person has finished speaking. You need to be interested in them and their responses. Avoid saying, "Yes" to them and immediately head off in another direction. If you agree with someone (or not) add a relevant comment about that point before moving on. It shows you were listening properly and have taken it in. Then you can change direction or the conversation easily. In a lot of cases, people aren't really listening to each other; they are just taking turns to speak.

Listening doesn't mean not talking. In fact, the best listeners are talking too. They are almost facilitating the conversation, asking clarifying questions (see questioning next), checking for understanding, responding with empathetic statements such as, "Wow, that must have really been a struggle for you" and at the very least nodding or giving non-verbal cues that they are engaged, comprehending and involved in the discussion that's occurring.

Reflective listening is when we are using questions to clarify our understanding or showing that we understand by using supportive statements.

Active listening is the use of non verbal responses such as nodding, eye contact or facial expressions or even encouraging verbal indicators such as "Uh huh, yes, wow etc."

In all of these areas of listening, pausing before your response should be a consideration. If we don't pause, we really aren't giving our brains an opportunity to let the other person's words sink in.

Questioning skills

Knowing how to ask the right questions can save time, create the right atmosphere and avoid slipping into a 'telling' mode. When people think about different types of questions, the standard responses are 'Open' and 'Closed'. Well, they are the two most basic types of questions, sure but there are others that can have an impact which are varieties of both the standard open and closed question types.

Let's look at the two basic questions first anyway:

OPEN questions start with:

- How
- Why
- Where
- What
- When
- Who

That's it. There aren't any other ways to start an open question. Why is it called an open question? Well, starting a question with one of these words is more likely to engage the other person to provide an answer that requires more than just a one word response. There's actually no real guarantee to that but the chances are much higher.

For example: "How do you think the session is going?" should open up the opportunity for the respondent to share their thoughts on the session. Of course, they could just say "Fine". That's when you would follow up with another open question such as, "What exactly do you think is fine about it?" which will give them more of a reason to share their thoughts.

CLOSED questions have a lot more ways of starting. Some examples include:

- Should
- Did
- Can
- Will
- Could
- Shall

Closed questions normally provide the respondent with the option of a one word response which is often 'Yes' or 'No'.

For example: "Can you write this down?" will mean the other person is going to either say 'Yes' or 'No'.

Knowing this basic information can help us in our coaching. If we want the person to share their thoughts and feelings on something – the obvious way to get them to talk or 'open up' is to ask an 'Open' question. If we want to clarify something, then a 'Closed' question will do it.

Then there are a number of other question types that can be applied to these Open or Closed questions. These include:

Leading Question – this is where you would ask a question towards a type of response you want to hear. For example, "What did you like about the presentation?" is effectively leading the other person to tell you what they liked about it. There isn't much room for another response unless they liked nothing about it at all. Of course you can have an open leading or a closed leading question.

Echoic Question – this is where you repeat back part of a statement to the person that just said something to you. This is especially useful if you didn't hear a part of their sentence or want to clarify a component of what they said. For example, if someone was giving you their address and you didn't hear the name of the street correctly, as in "I live at 245 'urrrmm' Street", you would respond by asking, "You live at 245 'what' street?" This tells the other person that you heard everything else okay – it was just the street name they need to repeat a bit more clearly.

Rhetorical Question – these are questions that don't require a response. They often don't sound like actual questions. For example, "I wonder what would happen if we all got sick at once?" Sometimes a rhetorical question is used just to get people to think about something rather than come up with an immediate solution or response.

Clarifying Question – Use these to check your understanding or to delve a bit deeper into a part of the discussion. These types of questions can be structured like, "Are you saying that they didn't care about what they did?" This will give the other person an opportunity to either confirm what you asked or clarify something different.

Direct Question – we don't often use direct questions. We tend to soften them up a bit. For example, the direct question, "Where's the bus station?" is often asked after a softener statement like, "Excuse me, I'm a little lost. Where's the bus station?"

Of course, you could actually ask a question in another way. For example, if you are struggling to get someone to open up and talk to you, try the phrase, "Tell me about..." This is not a question as such but acts like a question in getting them to talk to you. Try it out next time you need some help in getting someone to talk to you. I find this especially useful for my children. When I ask, "What did you do today?" They often respond with shrugged shoulders or the one word answer, "Stuff." Yet, when I change it to; "Tell me about your day." I get a little more information.

Paraphrasing

In order for us to ensure that we have understood someone correctly or for us to know whether someone has understood us correctly, we can use the communication tool known as paraphrasing. This is basically defined as saying something back to someone in our own words. It is not repeating verbatim. That only shows that we can copy what the other person has said. When we say it back in our own words, we have to internalise it and translate it into a way we may have said it.

Think about someone who has to communicate in a language foreign to their native language. They have to follow four steps:

1. They hear what is said in the foreign language
2. They translate what was said into their native language
3. They formulate their response in their native language
4. They translate their response into the foreign language

That's quite a task. It can be exhausting and it takes time. However, it helps to internalise what is said. This is the same as paraphrasing. We internalise what is said, translate it into our words and say it back again.

When we paraphrase, we give the other person a chance to confirm what we heard was what the other person meant to say. It's a simple act but it can save so much trouble. Taking an extra few seconds to ensure we have it right or that the person we are talking with has understood what we say can save time, errors and extra effort.

As far as communication goes, it's a tool that should be used much more often.

Tone of voice

All too often we focus on the words that we use rather than the way we use them. It's true that words are important. In the field of Law, if you don't read the 'fine print' – the words, then you could get into trouble. However, as you'll see in the 'Body Language' paragraphs following, the words only account for a small part of the impact of what is being said.

Let's take for example the phrase:

"Who did this?"

Now depending on how this is said, the reaction of those around will be quite different. If the phrase was said in a delighted tone, it's likely to bring everyone forward seeking to take the credit.

However, if the same phrase was said in an angry tone, you are likely to get the opposite response. If you're uncertain as to how this works, try it out at home. My kids tend to all rush in when the 'delighted' tone is used and hide when the 'angry' tone is employed.

There are many tones we can add too. Tones are ways of speaking and the list is pretty huge. Some examples include:

- Angry
- Happy
- Bored
- Amorous
- Embarrassed
- Sad
- Condescending

- Frustrated
- Amazed
- Confused
- Excited
- Friendly
- Anxious
- Scared

Why don't you practice saying a shopping list in different tones to someone and see if they can guess which tone you're using. They'll usually be right.

In a coaching situation, you can also change the whole meaning of a sentence by where you put the biggest emphasis. The intonation of the voice can alter meaning dramatically.

Take this sentence for example:

"I never said you could leave early"

It seems pretty harmless right?

Okay – let's look at changing the intonation (the emphasis) of each word in turn and look at what it does to the sentence:

Phrase	Means
"**I** never said you could leave early" –	someone may have said you could leave early but it wasn't me.
"I **never** said you could leave early" -	I deny ever saying that you could leave early.
"I never **said** you could leave early" -	I may have implied that you could leave early but didn't actually say it.
"I never said **you** could leave early" -	Someone else may be leaving early but not you.
"I never said you **could** leave early" -	We may have talked about leaving early but I never confirmed it.

"I never said you could **leave** early" - There may be something you could do early but it wasn't "leaving".

"I never said you could leave **early**" - You can leave alright but not early.

So, as you can see, the placement of the emphasis can alter the meaning of a simple seven word sentence a lot. Why is this important? Well it's not just about the way YOU say something – as in when you are speaking with someone – that's very important. It's also about how the other person takes what is said. So if you speak with a monotone voice (no change in pitch or variance) then emphasis can seemingly be nowhere and if you decide to write the feedback down – or send it by email, you open yourself up to the other person's interpretation. That can depend on their current state of mind, their setting, their last interaction with you – a whole host of different impacts. If you can read a simple seven word sentence seven different ways – imagine how many ways you could take a lengthy email on how your performance was going!

If you're going to give feedback – give it verbally. Use email only as confirmation. Feedback should always be a verbal process. It's the only way an exchange of understanding can take place.

Body language

When we communicate in a face to face setting, body language contributes the most to our communication. It's more than the tone of voice we use and the actual words we speak. In fact, the words we speak have the least value of all three components. In studies conducted in the 1960s by Albert Mehrabian, the statistics showed that 7% were attributed to Words, 38% to tone of voice and 55% to non verbal cues – such as body language or facial expression. In non face to face communication such as telephone communication, these figures change to 85% tone of voice and 7% words. *

With this information, we can completely alter our message by the way we say something. Let's take for example two separate tones of voice: angry and delighted. If I was to walk in the office and in an 'angry' tone say, "What's all this?" I am likely to get a totally different reaction than if I was to use the same words in a 'delighted' tone. In case of the angry tone, people are likely to remove themselves from the vicinity in case they get accused of being guilty of something. However, if I was to say the exact same words in a delighted tone, the chances are that people will come running to see if they can get some credit for something.

There is no doubt that the words are important but you can see how much the tone of voice can change the way those words can be taken. Adding to that, the way we look, stand, hold our arms, frown, smile, stomp up and down, play with our hair – everything physically will also add an angle on our wording.

In coaching, the use of all three components should be uniform; our words, our tone and our body language should all be contributing to the same message.

* - Mehrabian's studies actually referred to communication about feelings and attitudes. Although these statistics have been generally accepted for all communication, Mehrabian states on his website that they are only confirmed for the subject of his experiments. See www.kaaj.com/psych

Formal coaching

Planned coaching with an agenda will create some security and parameters for the individual being coached. It's important to set the expectation in these sessions so people are comfortable and not surprised. Try to set them at ease. Let them know in advance of what will take place wherever possible. Remember, you want those being coached to get something from this session. You want an improvement in behaviours. You want them to look forward to it so they need to see what's in it for them.

You may like to consider the following five steps in a formal coaching session:

1. Introduction

2. Agenda building

3. Discussion

4. Action point/plan

5. Summary

1. Introduction

Begin with a clear statement of why you are meeting

"Our meeting today is your (1st, 2nd, 3rd) discussion for this year...."

Then go on to outline what you will be doing.

"We will be reviewing the progress you are making towards..... and how you are using the coaching to help you achieve your customer service standards. It will mean looking at what you need to continue to do, do more of and stop doing..."

Follow this with a description of how you will conduct the discussion.

"We start by setting the agenda. We have one hour, and need to ensure we cover all the issues important to each of us. Once we've decided our agenda we'll discuss each item in turn. I'd like your views first and then I will give my views. After good discussion we'll agree whatever action needs taking and record the action points. I'd like you to record those and then summarise them at the end. That way, we can be sure that we agree on what has been discussed and what each of us needs to do. After the meeting I'll need a copy of the action points"

2. Agenda Building

Try drafting in advance of the session. Don't forget to review action points from your last coaching session.

If you haven't reviewed the previous coaching session, make sure it is completed before starting the discussion.

"Let's start by building the agenda. What topics or issues do you have? (They list them) I'd like to talk about ………. plus………."

If the agenda is a long one, you might have to set some priorities in order to manage them.

"It looks as if we may have more here than we can deal with right now. I would definitely like to cover…what are your priority items? Ok then we'll talk about…plus the others if we have time. Otherwise we'll set another meeting."

3. Discussion

With each item on the agenda ask for your staff member's views first. With an open question invite them to, for example, talk about what they've been particularly pleased with.

Ask questions and probe for further clarification before giving your views. Once you understand their views, ask for suggestions and actions.

Explore important issues – give them the necessary time

Make sure that you give positive feedback when you can. *"I particularly liked the way you …."*

Don't avoid problems. Take a joint problem solving approach. Analyse what happened and why things happened, without judging. What learning needs to take place from the problem?

What action points are needed for improvement?

Use the competencies to suggest how things could be done differently.

"The problem we've identified links directly to these categories in the performance standards. Taking more time to ...."

4. Action Points

Ensure that each agenda item results in action and that the staff member records this.

"What do you think you need to do to make sure that doesn't happen again? Make a note that I need to provide you........."

Action points should be concise, relevant and easy to apply. You could use the acronym:

SMART:

Specific – actual statements of what needs to happen eg: *"On each phone call with the customer, I will ask their permission to ask the validation questions as a lead in rather than just asking them with no introduction."*

Measurable – We will review this in our phone call observations each week and see if it's happening

Achievable – You have received the training and know how to do it

Relevant – This will help you in your role and make an impact on both your performance and the experience of the customer

Time Bound – You will start immediately and we will check on it weekly

Together these points form the action plan – which is then available for monitoring at the next performance discussion.

5. Summary

At the end of the discussion phase, ask the staff member to summarise.

Use the summary to ensure that the action points are clear and agreed to by you both.

Identify any leftover items or issues that need later discussion.

Remind the staff member to give you a copy of the action points.

70:30 discussion in coaching where you only do the 30% of the talking as the coach – remember the key element of self discovery

It's important not to cancel scheduled coaching sessions. Doing so sends a signal that the individual is less important than whatever activity or person has 'bumped' them off the schedule. Try everything you can to follow through on planned coaching sessions.

Advantages of Formal Coaching:

- It's scheduled so it should happen

- It's planned so there is a structure to follow

- It's regular, so follow up is built in and scheduled

- There are parameters set so expectations are easy to understand

- You should be away from the working area so it's easier to both give full attention

The GROW Model

The GROW model is another coaching technique which was developed in the United Kingdom in the 1980s. It's still a popular coaching model used today. It's simple, effective and easy to remember.

The four stages of the GROW model are:

- Goal
- Reality
- Options / Obstacles
- Way forward.

The Goal is the end point - where you need to be at the conclusion of the time period you are working on. This is why the goal needs to be SMART so there is no ambiguity about what is to be achieved, by when.

The Reality is the gap between the current situation and where the goal is. This is best looked at as a self-assessment from the team member being coached. This needs to be real and clear. You may need to help them understand exactly what the gap is. You may like to help set a number of steps in place to be achieved on the way to the goal. It's easier to achieve small steps rather than one huge one.

Options can then be discussed to look at ways to overcome any obstacles. Discuss and offer options that could be considered. This is a great place to ask powerful questions like, "What do you think you will need to change to actually achieve this goal?"

The Way Forward is to decide upon the next steps, identify what support is needed and include review dates and possibilities. Ensure you end positively.

Informal coaching

Unlike formal coaching, informal coaching can be done anytime and anywhere. It's normally impromptu or casual in its set up. We may still have a set time to sit with our teams or to 'walk the floor' but we may not have a series of things to mention, bring up or discuss. Informal coaching is not about correcting mistakes. How much nicer would environments at work be if we tried to catch people 'doing things right' rather than the usual 'correct mistakes'.

Informal coaching can have a greater impact than formal coaching because it is immediate. If you consider the time / impact curve (Fig 3 overleaf), the shorter the time has elapsed, the greater the impact is on the outcome. The longer you wait to comment on someone's behaviour, the less the impact will be. If you can say to someone immediately after a great sales call or a fantastic customer interaction that they did a terrific job, it will mean more than when you mention something in a formal meeting two weeks later.

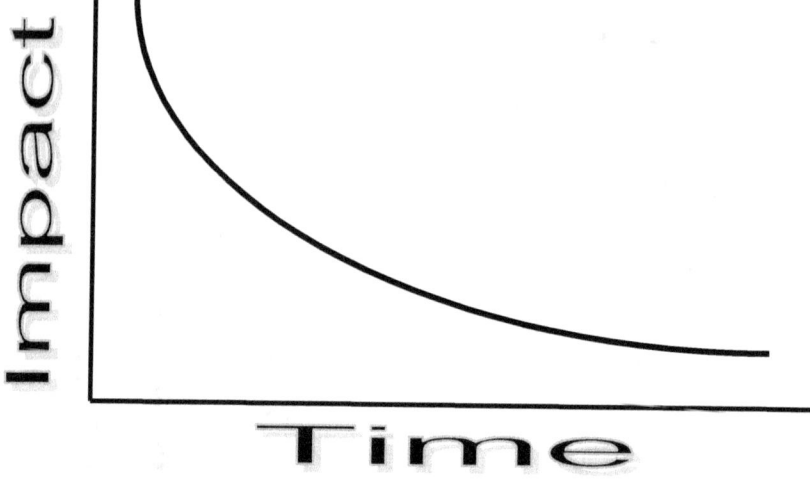

Fig 3. Time Impact Curve

Informal coaching can happen anytime. By its very name, informal means that there will unlikely be a regular set of rules or guidelines. Coaching of this nature can happen just about anytime, anywhere. You don't need (and probably shouldn't) start a conversation of informal coaching by mentioning anything about coaching. It's normally best to happen in the flow of a conversation or in the spontaneous moment.

You can informally coach someone as you walk past their desk, or as you walk the floor generally, as you leave a sales call with them, as you chat over the water cooler, as you talk in the elevator or as they come to your office about something. The good thing about this is that there are no real rules. Use the techniques described earlier in the book under the 10 Key Principles of Coaching.

Advantages of Informal Coaching:

- It's brief and requires little or no planning

- You can correct mistakes instantly and avoid them being repeated

- It's immediate and has a far greater impact than a delayed response

- It can be done anytime, anywhere

- Doesn't have to be done under the banner of 'coaching'

- It can be totally impromptu

Remote coaching

In today's world you are very likely to find yourself in a position where you can't coach or meet your team members in the same space. This may be due to a pandemic situation like that experienced in the first half of 2020 or you may have team members spread far and wide. For these or other reasons you may need to engage in coaching remotely. For some managers these days, remote coaching is the only option available to them. If your staff members engage with customers on the phone, then remote coaching can be a great way to see how they perform using that medium. You can identify if they are prepared or easily distracted and unlike scenarios you may role play with them face to face, you are focusing on their tone and voice elements much more which can be very useful if the telephone is the method they use to perform their task.

In any event, knowing a few key skills on remote coaching can help in your role – especially if you don't want to have to wait until the next time you are physically meeting with someone to offer feedback or to coach them. This is very useful if you need to address something that needs immediate attention. Don't neglect the other skills discussed in this book. They are all relevant while coaching remotely.

There are several mediums for remote coaching including the telephone, video conferencing like Microsoft teams or Zoom, Skype, Instant Messenger etc. Video conferencing gives you the benefit of seeing and hearing the other person. Skype and other 'internet chat' options can drastically reduce the effectiveness of the communication as you lose both the physical language (unless you have a camera or web cam attached) and the audio language components. Look back at the chapter on communication to see how this can drastically affect the meaning of a sentence.

Remote coaching on the telephone can sometimes be easier in some respects. Some people find it easy to develop rapport and even trust on the telephone as it's a tool people use a lot of in their lives. It's important though not to slip into too much of an informal mode. You can lose some of the key elements of a good coaching session by treating a phone conversation as less important. Remember to consider having an agenda, a set time to talk, items to discuss and two-way communication. Always take the opportunity to follow up with an email to confirm actions and details of the conversation. A good old-fashioned telephone call may be a good way to break up th seemingly endless waves of video conferencing meetings as well.

Try using a headset or some hands free operation. This leaves you free to takes notes and write things down, refer to notes etc. Don't try to hold a coaching session on the phone while you're driving though. It's potentially dangerous and at the very least you will be distracted and lose out on some of your key listening skills. It's obvious too that you shouldn't be 'multitasking' yourself and trying to check texts and emails etc while you're coaching someone on the phone. You need to be 'present' and concentrating on the person and your conversation.

As you aren't able to 'see' body language, your speaking and listening skills are more important in these settings. Ensure that you both paraphrase and encourage paraphrasing to confirm understanding. You can also develop the skill of 'hearing' the body language of the other person. You can hear if the person is being animated in their speech, if they are waving their arms around, smiling, tutting or even eating while they're in conversation with you.

Ensure that you allow silences to happen. It sounds more awkward on the telephone than face to face but you need to allow the other person time to think. You may have the experience yourself when someone explains something to you and asks immediately afterwards – "Well, what do you think?" Of course, you were listening right up until that point and then you're supposed to give an answer without processing it? No, we need time to process information, so allow those silences to happen.

You can continue to use the ten key points of coaching explained earlier. They are all still valid in remote coaching. Giving feedback, helping the other person self discover and do most of the talking etc are all important elements of coaching whether it's remote or face to face.

Barriers to coaching

There may be some objections raised by staff to coaching. Some are quite valid from their perspective, so it's a good idea to be armed with some good counter reasoning in order to solve and overcome the barriers.

Here are some of the barriers to coaching and potential solutions in dealing with them:

Barrier	Solution
Age (you may be younger than them)	Get them on your side. Acknowledge that you value their experience in the organisation or life. Offer to receive feedback as well as give it. Ask for their help. Explain that although you're young, you have studied, practiced, learnt, researched – whatever it is you have done to deserve the role you're in.

Barrier	Solution
Age (you may be older than them)	Acknowledge that you are of an older generation and your views on things may differ – especially preferences in music etc. Play to your strengths. You have a wealth of experience. You've made mistakes and learnt a lot. You bring stability, experience and knowledge.
Bad experience in the past	Acknowledge that sometimes coaching isn't always a great experience. Ask them to share it with you. Share a similar one if you've had it. Ask them to share their expectation of coaching and what they would like to see. Explain to them yours and ask them to trust you and prove your value.
Never been coached	Ask them to share what they would like to get out of coaching. Reassure them that it's a positive experience. Share what you have gained from being coached and why you like to coach. Explain that coaching is where improvements happen and the benefits to them.
New to the company	Although you're new to the company, you bring with you specific leadership / coaching skills that qualify you for this

	role. Ask for their help in getting to understand the company products / services / systems etc. You were hired for your coaching and leadership skills, not for your company knowledge.
No action	Here's where the person says all the right things but doesn't change. Put in small, quick measures of accountability. Shorten the time span and follow up soon after. Ask the hard questions – "You said you would do this, why haven't you?" Don't offer excuses for them. Ensure they come up with the actions – don't set the measures – let them do it.
Repeated poor behaviour	Ensure they have had adequate training and opportunities to practice. Go back at looking at the cause for the behaviour. Put in positive consequences for improvements and, negative consequences for continuing poor behaviour. Ask them to give reasons for the behaviour. Ask them what they would do if they were in your shoes and had to deal with them.

Dealing with difficult behaviours

People naturally have a defence mechanism built into them commonly known as the 'fight or flight' response. It's that moment when you make a split decision to either fight and make a stand or run away to fight another day. Although our process time to think things through may have provided us with a different (and sometimes better) response, our immediate 'under pressure' response can be quite out of character and even damaging.

This response is caused by what's known as the amygdala hijack which is a term attributed to Daniel Goleman in his 1996 book "*Emotional Intelligence: Why It Can Matter More Than IQ*". In the book, the term is used to describe emotional responses from people which are out of measure with the actual threat because it has triggered a much more significant emotional threat. In other words, the emotional reaction to what is in front of you has triggered something of greater emotional importance. Often we hear of people 'over reacting' and that is often due to their emotional understanding of a particular event being greater than our own.

The main types of responses can be put into three categories: fight, flight and freeze. When coaching someone and especially while giving feedback, people already put themselves in a higher emotional state. The things spoken about hit personal registers and put people under pressure so you can often come up against the following:

Fight response

People tend to get angry, argumentative, stop listening, are stubborn or even sarcastic. When experiencing this response, we might say something like:

"Don't speak to me like that!" or

"If you don't calm down I'll terminate the call"

Flight response

People here tend to want to avoid conflict, blame someone else, blame a system fault, or pass the buck in general. When experiencing this response, we might say:

"One of the others must have told you that"

"It's not my problem"

"So you want to talk to the manager, then?"

Freeze response

Here's where your mind goes blank, you can't think of anything to say or you feel embarrassed.

The thing about the amygdala hijack is that it's automatic but we can control it. While our brain (cortex) is accessing its records for an appropriate response, the amygdale also receives the information and offers a shortcut immediate threat response and blocks off the 'slow thinking'. Our response to a situation will affect the outcome. If we think of the outcome in these terms: Outcome = Event + Response or written the other way: Event (E) = my response to the event, (R) = the outcome, then we know that:

E – things that will happen

R – how I choose to respond to it

O – will determine the outcome or result

As an example: If a staff member calls me names (E) and I get offended and shout back at them (R), then the outcome (O) is going to be conflict between us.

But...

If a staff member calls me names (E) and I ignore the name calling, keep calm and stick to the facts (R), then the outcome is going to be a more logical and productive discussion between us (O)

So, how I manage my response or reaction to things and people can determine the end result I want to get. It all sounds straight forward and actually is. The simple four step process to remember in each case of potential conflict is:

1. Pause

2. Listen and acknowledge the response or the behaviour

3. Return to the facts

4. Focus on a solution

Here are a few examples of what can happen and how using this approach can assist. Let's take it that you are giving someone feedback on getting to work late:

Coaching and Feedback Made Easy   79

Event	Response
Staff member cries	1. PAUSE
	2. The aim of this discussion is not to upset you...
	3.We are here to talk about the fact that you have been getting to work late
	4. Tell me why this is happening?
Staff member is aggressive (e.g. says something like: you are such a bad manager)	1. PAUSE
	2. This discussion is not about me...
	3. We are here to talk about the fact that you have been getting to work late
	4. We need to agree how you are going to manage to get to work on time.
Staff member is defensive (e.g. why are you picking on me?)	1. PAUSE
	2. I am not picking on you...
	3. The fact is, you have got to work more than 10 minutes late on the last 3 days
	4. Tell me why this is happening?
Staff member blames (e.g. I'm not the only one in the team who is doing it)	1. PAUSE
	2. If it is happening with others, you can know that I will

address it with them. Or what happens in other managers departments is not my issue. In this department, I expect my staff to get to work on time.

3, We are here to talk about your lateness, so...

4. Tell me why this is happening?

Staff member is silent	1. PAUSE
	2. If you don't talk to me, we cannot work together to fix it...
	3. As I mentioned, you have been late the last 3 days.
	4. Why is that?

So, what we can see from these examples is that in each case, you can manage the response by:

1. Pausing (to manage the amygdala hijack)

2. Not taking things personally (reminding yourself that it was an attempt to divert your attention)

3. Sticking to the facts

4. Keeping the conversation moving forward to a solution.

Summary

Coaching and giving feedback really depends on the attitude of you as the coach and of the person being coached. Unless you have their buy-in, you are unlikely to make any real change in their behaviour or strike any desire to change. Motivation for change is the key to the success. Remember that external motivation is short lived. Creating an internal desire and therefore internal motivation brings about the best and longer lasting changes.

Focus on what the person being coached is motivated by and work round your discussion to outline the benefits to them in a way they will understand and accept.

This book isn't a complete guide to all coaching and feedback answers and techniques, so spend time researching the topic further, talk over your experiences with others and continuously look for ways to improve your abilities as well as ways to improve your teams.

As a coach, you should also consider having a coach. Receiving another person's perspective on how we coach and approach our role can be very valuable.

Good luck in your coaching and feedback role. If you have found this book to be useful, we'd love to hear from you.

Derek Good Bio

Derek is an author, actor, presenter, facilitator, voice over artist, husband, father of four children and currently a director of LearningPlanet Limited which helps improve the productivity of organisations and the confidence of their staff through sales, service and leadership skills in bite-sized videos and short training modules.

Derek is a facilitator who works with leadership teams in LEGO Serious Play, TMI profiling, problem solving and strategy sessions.

He was previously the Managing Director of Rapid Results - a leading New Zealand training and consultancy firm specialising in contact centres. There he was responsible for spearheading customer relationships programmes and managed all the sales and communications functions for the business.

Derek has over twenty years' experience in general management in the UK and New Zealand market, is an Author of several books on leadership, coaching, sales, Return on investment, training activities and humour. He has also been a past winner in the Westpac Enterprise Auckland North Shore Business Excellence Awards and the TUANZ innovation award for Education.

Other books available from Derek Good:

Remote Activities for Virtual Teams by Derek Good & Craig McFadyen

Paperback and Kindle: 224 Pages

First published 2020

ISBN-13: 979-8640744965
ASIN: B0884FFGFC

101 Training Activities and How to Run Them by Derek Good & Craig McFadyen

Paperback & Kindle: 254 pages

First Published: 2018

ISBN-10: 1987708784
ISBN-13: 978-1987708783

Practical Leadership by Derek Good

Paperback & Kindle: 172 pages

First Published: 2015

ISBN-10: 1512311650

ISBN-13: 978-1512311655

Leading a Team by Derek Good

Paperback: 104 pages
First Published: 2012
ISBN-13: 978-1478332039
ISBN-10: 1478332034

ROI: The sales person's secret weapon by Derek Good

Paperback: 56 pages
First Published: 2011
ISBN-10: 1463764634
ISBN-13: 978-1463764630

Return on Investment Made Easy by Derek Good & Craig McFadyen

Paperback: 108 pages
First Published: 2010
ISBN-10: 1452835993
ISBN-13: 978-1452835990